LET'S START A COMMUNITY CAMPAIGN

TAKING CIVIC ACTI

Sadie Silva

CIVICS FOR THE REAL WORLD™

Rosen Classroom™

Published in 2019 by The Rosen Publishing Group, Inc.
29 East 21st Street, New York, NY 10010

Book Design: Rachel Rising
Editor: Ryan Wolf

Photo Credits: Cover Rawpixel.com/Shutterstock.com; p. 4 wk1003mike/Shutterstock.com; p. 7 imtmphoto/Shutterstock.com; p. 8 Syda Productions/Shutterstock.com; p. 11 D.Somsup/Shutterstock.com; p. 12 LightField Studios/Shutterstock.com; p. 14 BIGANDT.COM/Shutterstock.com.

ISBN: 9781538365694
6-pack ISBN: 9781538365700

Manufactured in the United States of America

CPSIA Compliance Information: Batch #WS18RC: For Further Information contact Rosen Publishing, New York, New York at 1-800-237-9932

CONTENTS

MAKING THINGS BETTER

Do you ever want to change things? Maybe you think your neighborhood playground needs new swings because the old ones are broken. Maybe you think your street isn't safe because drivers go too fast. You might think there's nothing you can do. But even kids can make a difference.

You can start a community campaign! This is when people work together to try to fix a problem or change something.

WHERE TO START?

The first thing you can do is talk to other people in your neighborhood. See if they agree with you. Ask them to help you make a difference and fix the problem. Be **polite** and respectful. Not everyone will agree with you. That's okay!

The next step is to find out who can fix the problem. Communities have officials who help keep things running. Ask your parents or teachers to help you figure out who can help.

IT TAKES A COMMUNITY

Different people in your neighborhood may have different ways to help the campaign. If you all have a meeting, you can figure out who can do what. Maybe one of your friends is good at writing! She can start working on letters or **petitions**. Maybe your neighbor knows someone in local government. He can ask them for advice. It will be important to come to a **consensus** about the right thing to do.

SPEAKING AND WRITING

Letters and petitions are very important. They tell officials why something should be changed. Show your best writing and use good manners. Tell the person you're writing to what you want to change and why it's a good idea.

People can also go to government meetings. Many meetings include a chance for citizens to stand up and tell officials why they should make certain changes. It's good to speak up!

DON'T GIVE UP

It might feel like no one is listening to you. But sometimes change takes time. Officials probably need to talk about and vote on any changes. If the change will take money, they will need to figure out where that money will come from. You can keep going to meetings or writing letters to ask what's going on. Be **patient**, but don't give up! Keep asking for answers.

CHANGE STARTS WITH YOU

Not every community campaign will work. Sometimes there are reasons why officials can't make changes right away or at all. If there are good reasons, you may have to change your **goal** or wait a while.

Maybe you'll need help to understand the reasons. If no one gives you the reasons or the reasons don't make sense, you can persist, or continue onward. Change has to start somewhere! Why not with you?

GLOSSARY

consensus: General agreement among a group's members.

goal: Something you're trying to do or accomplish.

patient: Able to stay calm when waiting for something or when dealing with a problem.

petition: A written request, or question, asking a government or person to do something.

polite: Showing good manners and respect for others.

INDEX